LOCKED

UP...

NOTED.

Copyright 2019 Angelbrite Liberte

This Journal Belongs to:

www.ingramcontent.com/pod-product-compliance
Lightning Source LLC
Chambersburg PA
CBHW021823170526
45157CB00007B/2671